Stay "Safe"

Written by Isaiah Mulligan

Illustrated by Francheska Acevedo

This

one

is

for

the

culture.

Life says stay safe Aakeem,
but no one really wants me to be
safe.

Watch your back Aakeem!
Be careful out there!
Stay out of trouble.
Be Safe!!!
Stay safe!

I follow every rule on the road.
I do not speed, follow the lights,
safety first, so why do
cops stop me still?

Clothes do not define me
as a person, so why do people
look at me when I wear
my hoodie?

My mother says your
name gives you identity, so why
do they call me other names
to bring me down?

ULLIGAN
RKETING INC.
#?@%
Yum-Yum
COLA

I work hard because they say
hard work leads to success,
so why when I go on interviews
and say my name, I automatically
feel my application being
denied.

Hm, well qualified, but I don't know about that name.
MR. PICKLES

I have early mornings and
leave late nights from work,
continuously trying to prove I belong.
I play a critical role in our network,
so why don't they promote me
when I work as hard as my
colleague sitting
next to me?

MULLIGAN
MARKETING INC.
MULLIGAN
MARKETING INC.
Wow, Todd and Aakeem's project is doing amazing!
Yeah, great job Todd!
Thanks boss!

Life teaches us that our history
makes us who we are and
shapes our past, present, and future;
so why do they only teach me
about the people who owned my
ancestors and not about
the black kings and queens who
shaped my history and a
mere mention of them in February.

As you are all aware, it is now February which is Black History month. Put away your notes on Ceasar, we are starting a new unit on Dr. Martin Luther King Jr.
Dr. Martin Luth
Nurse
Restroom

Skin tone does not measure
character and hard work,
or even the love I can share
with someone else; so why can't I
marry who I want to
without being judged?

So this is who you are marrying?
Yes, mom!

I save every cent I make,
so why can't I afford to still live in
neighborhoods like yours?

I'm sorry, but this is something out of your price range.

I was not raised like all,
but I am still educated and successful
in my own way; so why does how I
dress or speak make you feel
like you know
who I am?

'Dope'?! Homeboy, you gonna buy something or what?
Check out this car I want.
Wow, I like it. It's dope!

Safety is important to me
just like everyone else, but why
do I get stopped when I am
at an airport every time?

Uh, sir. I'm gonna need you to come back to security check.
Dippinn' Donuts

It is not until we work
together that I
can be
safe.

Truly safe and truly
be who I
want to be.

I can be whoever I want. I can do anything.

Sincerely, Aakeem.

The Creative Minds

Isaiah Mulligan is a South Bronx native. He graduated from Emmanuel College with a bachelor's in Business Management. After graduating, Isaiah served 2 years in Americorps doing nonprofit work in Boston, MA. During these years, Isaiah was exposed to his love of education, beginning his journey of being an educator. He spent 3 years teaching in Boston, MA as a Kindergarten and 1st grade teacher. He later moved to the DMV area, where he spent 2 years teaching 1st grade ELA. Isaiah has always had a love for writing ever since he was a young boy. He was excited to write this piece because it was based off of experiences people of color continuously go through and wants to push race and equity conservations with youth.

Isaiah Mulligan

Francheska Acevedo (F.ACE) is a freelance art from Providence, Rhode Island. She graduated from the University of Rhode Island with a bachelor's in Arts and Communications. She still resides in Providence. Francheska is primarily a digital artist, but does like to paint on occasion. Francheska's art is influenced by the cartoons she watched as a child, which various popular artists such as Kaws, Alex Solis, and Lauren YS ect. The harsh humor of her three older brothers, Renso, Chris and Tony also have influenced Francheska's art as well. She hopes to one day have her work seen everywhere from tee shirts, paintings hung in galleries, and on tv. For now, she is slowly building a name for herself one project at a time.

Francheska Acevedo